Table of Contents

The World of the Dinosaurs

The world has changed a great deal since the days of the dinosaurs. They lived during the earth's "Middle Years". This was a time when great changes took place on the earth's surface. The "Middle Years", or **Mesozoic** (MEZ-uh-ZO-ik) **Era** as it is called, were divided into three periods. In these three periods, the continents of the earth were in different places, and different kinds of dinosaurs lived in each time.

The Super-continent

If we went back 225 million years, we would be at the beginning of the first age of dinosaurs—the **Triassic** (Try-AH-sik) **Period**. In these early years, the world's land was not in separate continents as it is today. All of the land was joined together in one 'super-**continent**' called **Pangaea** (Pan-JEE-uh). This huge mass of land went almost all the way around the earth, between the North and South Poles. The **climate** of this continent was very warm and comfortable for the first dinosaurs and their ancestors. They could also travel quite widely, as far as the supply of food would take them.

Something was happening, however, that would soon break up Pangaea. The earth is made up of plates. These plates are always shifting. The movement is so slow that we don't usually notice it. But sometimes the earth reminds us with shattering earthquakes! By 150 million years ago, the single land mass had separated into two continents—**Laurasia** in the north, and **Gondwanaland** in the south. This split happened during the second age of dinosaurs, which is called the **Jurassic** (Jer-AS-sick) **Period**. Even though there were now two continents, dinosaurs might still have been able to travel between them on bridges of land.

The last age of the dinosaurs is called the **Cretaceous** (Kreh-TAY-shus) **Period**. By its end, the continents had moved almost to the same spots where they are now. This great movement of land probably meant that the climate changed for the animals on the continents. The temperature would have been cooler as the pieces of land moved farther north or south. All of this movement took a very long time. In the meantime, many different kinds of dinosaurs lived successfully all over the world.

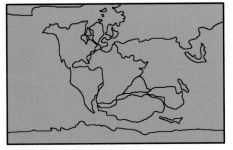
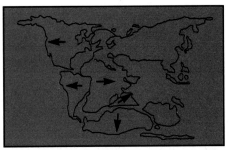
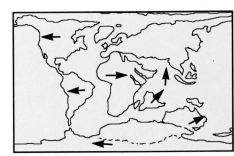

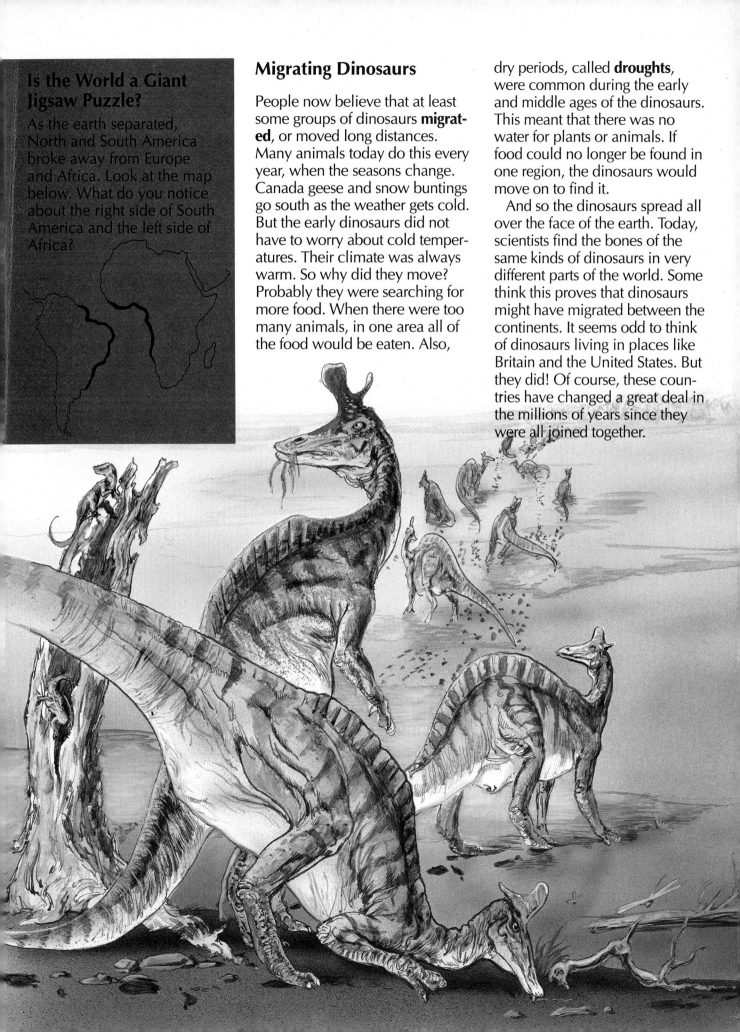

Is the World a Giant Jigsaw Puzzle?

As the earth separated, North and South America broke away from Europe and Africa. Look at the map below. What do you notice about the right side of South America and the left side of Africa?

Migrating Dinosaurs

People now believe that at least some groups of dinosaurs **migrated**, or moved long distances. Many animals today do this every year, when the seasons change. Canada geese and snow buntings go south as the weather gets cold. But the early dinosaurs did not have to worry about cold temperatures. Their climate was always warm. So why did they move? Probably they were searching for more food. When there were too many animals, in one area all of the food would be eaten. Also, dry periods, called **droughts**, were common during the early and middle ages of the dinosaurs. This meant that there was no water for plants or animals. If food could no longer be found in one region, the dinosaurs would move on to find it.

And so the dinosaurs spread all over the face of the earth. Today, scientists find the bones of the same kinds of dinosaurs in very different parts of the world. Some think this proves that dinosaurs might have migrated between the continents. It seems odd to think of dinosaurs living in places like Britain and the United States. But they did! Of course, these countries have changed a great deal in the millions of years since they were all joined together.

Living beside the Dinosaurs

The dinosaurs did not live alone on the earth. Let's look back about 150 million years and see what kinds of plants and animals lived alongside the dinosaurs.

Ancient Plants

In a lot of ways, the plant life was much like it is today in some parts of the world. You would recognize green leafy ferns, horsetails, club mosses, and the palm-like **cycads**. **Coniferous** trees, such as the spruce and pine that bear cones, also lived side by side with the dinosaurs. You would probably be more surprised by what you didn't see than what you did see. Flowering plants and trees, as well as grass, did not appear until the last age of the dinosaurs.

If you could somehow travel through the skies of this ancient world, you would look down on some familiar scenes. Seashore, marshes, swamps, forests, and plains—some of them quite dry—were all home to the animals of the Mesozoic Period. Many kinds of dinosaurs ate only plants. They evolved special features that made it possible for them to live on the kinds of plant life that surrounded them.

Dinosaur Diet

Scientists know a lot about what kinds of food certain species of dinosaurs ate. Some animals have been found with seeds in their stomachs that show the kinds of plants they ate. The teeth of these animals also tell us a lot about their diet. Some were made for ripping and shredding. Others were made for grinding and chewing. Can you tell which of these teeth was made for eating plants and which was for eating meat?

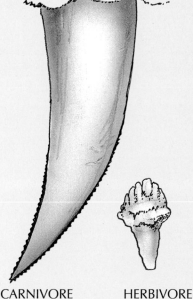

CARNIVORE   HERBIVORE

Other Creatures

It's easy to think that dinosaurs would be the only animals alive on earth because of their great size and numbers. But they were only one group of a wide range of animals that lived on land and in the ocean at this time. Distant relatives of many of today's creatures were among them.

In the waters, fish first appeared about 500 million years ago. That was long before the dinosaurs first stalked the earth. Some of the ancient fish were huge and fearsome monsters themselves. Today's sharks would seem small and tame by comparison. During the Cretaceous Period, two main groups of reptiles also lived in the seas. One was the **ichthyosaurs** (IK-thee-uh-SORES), a group that looked like today's dolphins. The other was the **plesiosaurs** (PLEH-sea-uh-sores) which were like the dinosaurs but swam with strong, paddle-like flippers. Their lower bodies looked much like the giant turtles that swam alongside them. The oceans were also filled with primitive jellyfish, corals, and shellfish such as clams.

Somewhere between water and land lived the **amphibians**. Among these creatures were the ancestors of the modern frogs. There were also some kinds of newts that are with us today, almost unchanged. But not all of these early amphibians would be familiar. Like their dry-land relatives, amphibians of long ago were often much larger. One creature, **_Mastodonsaurus_** (MASS-tuh-don-SORE-us), looked something like a cross between a frog and a crocodile. Its skull alone measured 1.4 metres (4.5 ft).

If you think that these enormous amphibians must have needed a lot of insects to fill up on, guess again. Some dragonflies of the time measured 75 centimetres (30 in) from wing tip to wing tip! Cockroaches grew up to 30 centimetres (1 ft) long! In spite of their huge size, the insects would have been the most recognizable group for a visitor from modern times. Two-thirds of all the insect types alive today shared the planet with the dinosaurs.

And what about our own ancestors, the land mammals? For about seventy million years, a group of mammal-like reptiles ruled the land. These had come from the reptiles of the ocean. The long and successful reign of these creatures was put to an end by the rise of the dinosaurs. They just could not compete against this powerful new group. But small descendants of theirs did manage to survive along with the dinosaurs. These were little animals much like today's mice or shrews, and were the world's first true mammals. They were called **synapsids** (sin-AP-sids).

Other animals that shared the land with the dinosaurs were more closely related to them. Snakes, crocodiles, lizards, and tortoises could all be found in much the same forms as we see them today.

7

What came before the Dinosaurs?

Where did these wondrous creatures come from? Did they simply appear one day, perfectly adapted to their surroundings and ready to rule the world? Not at all. Dinosaurs were the result of millions of years of **evolution** —nature's way of adapting animals to their **environment.**

All creatures alive today, came to be through a long, slow process of **adaptation**. This meant that their ancestors developed special features, little by little, that helped them survive. One generation, or set of parents, passed on its advantages to its children. Those that could not adapt died out.

Nature's Tricks

Nature depends on some strange tricks to give certain species an edge. For example, many plants have developed special features to attract insects, whose bodies will carry the plants' pollen on to other plants. The stapelia plant shown here smells like rotting meat to attract flies. These adaptations help the plants to reproduce, but do not make them very popular with gardeners!

In the Beginning...

All life on earth started with single-celled creatures. These slowly evolved into simple animals with many cells, such as worms and jellyfish, and later into hard-shelled animals like crabs. These early creatures are called invertebrates, meaning they had no backbones. It took about 3000 million years of development from the beginning of life to the appearance of the first fish. Fish were the first vertebrates, or creatures with backbones.

Some fish developed lungs, and so they were able to stay on dry land for certain periods. The first amphibians evolved from these. From the amphibians came the early reptiles—the first animals to live completely on land. Many people think that all large, ancient reptiles were dinosaurs. But dinosaurs were only one group that developed from these early reptiles. Others included animals like ichthyosaurs and plesiosaurs, that returned to the sea, as well as turtles and tortoises.

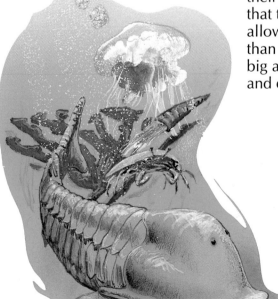

On Dry Land

Two groups of land animals came from the early reptiles: the mammal-like synapsids, which we saw earlier, and a group called the **diapsids** (die-AP-sids). Scientists gave the reptile families these names because of the different holes they had in their skulls. The diapsids had two holes in their skulls, behind the eye sockets. By the time the diapsids appeared, nature was getting very close to the first dinosaurs! The diapsids developed into two different groups. One became snakes and lizards. The other became the **archosaurs** (ARK-uh-SORES)— the "ruling reptiles".

In the first part of the dinosaur age, the dinosaurs themselves were not the most dominant group of archosaurs. Instead, their "grandparents", the **thecodonts** (THEK-uh-DONTS), ruled the earth. These crocodile-like animals, developed a new way of walking. Other animals of that time could not move very quickly because their limbs pointed outwards from their bodies. The thecodonts were able to draw their legs underneath them so that they did not sprawl. This allowed them to move faster than other reptiles. Speed is a big advantage in catching food and escaping from enemies.

DIAPSIDS

SYNAPSIDS

EARTH HISTORY CALENDAR

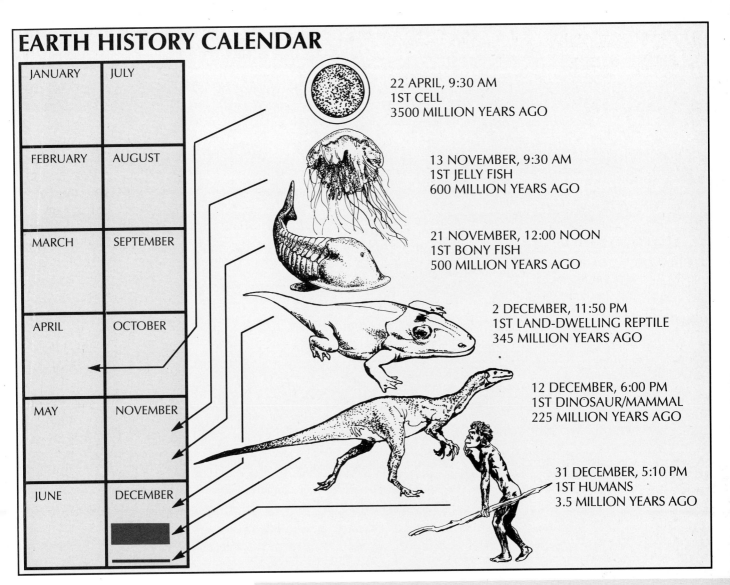

JANUARY	JULY
FEBRUARY	AUGUST
MARCH	SEPTEMBER
APRIL	OCTOBER
MAY	NOVEMBER
JUNE	DECEMBER

22 APRIL, 9:30 AM
1ST CELL
3500 MILLION YEARS AGO

13 NOVEMBER, 9:30 AM
1ST JELLY FISH
600 MILLION YEARS AGO

21 NOVEMBER, 12:00 NOON
1ST BONY FISH
500 MILLION YEARS AGO

2 DECEMBER, 11:50 PM
1ST LAND-DWELLING REPTILE
345 MILLION YEARS AGO

12 DECEMBER, 6:00 PM
1ST DINOSAUR/MAMMAL
225 MILLION YEARS AGO

31 DECEMBER, 5:10 PM
1ST HUMANS
3.5 MILLION YEARS AGO

In the Air

The dinosaurs were not the only kinds of animals that came from the thecodonts. Crocodiles evolved at about this time and have stayed much the same ever since. A group of flying reptiles, called the **pterosaurs** (TAIR-uh-sores) were also "children" of the thecodonts. Even though pterosaurs had wings, they were not the ancestors of our modern birds. The pterosaurs became extinct along with the dinosaurs. They have no living relatives today. Birds most likely did develop from **reptiles**, but from a different branch of the family tree.

How long is a Long Time?

Let's imagine history as a calendar. If we could squeeze all of earth's development into one year, the first sign of life—the single-celled bacteria and algae—would have appeared at 9:30 am on 22 April. In our model, it took almost seven months for life to go from there to produce the first backboned fish. These first arrived at noon on 21 November. The dinosaurs appeared at 6:00 pm on 12 December and died out at 5:00 pm on 25 December. Human beings are just babies compared to the dinosaurs. Our earliest ancestors only go back to 5:10 pm on 31 December. We've been around for less than seven hours!

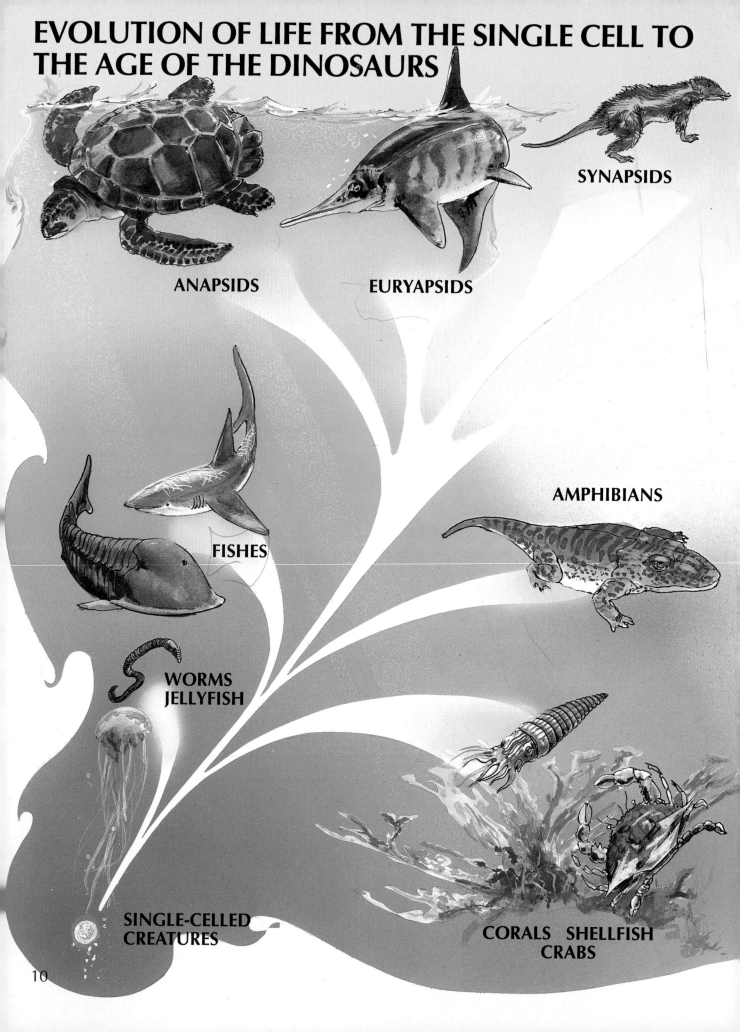

EVOLUTION OF LIFE FROM THE SINGLE CELL TO THE AGE OF THE DINOSAURS

SYNAPSIDS

ANAPSIDS

EURYAPSIDS

AMPHIBIANS

FISHES

WORMS
JELLYFISH

SINGLE-CELLED
CREATURES

CORALS   SHELLFISH
CRABS

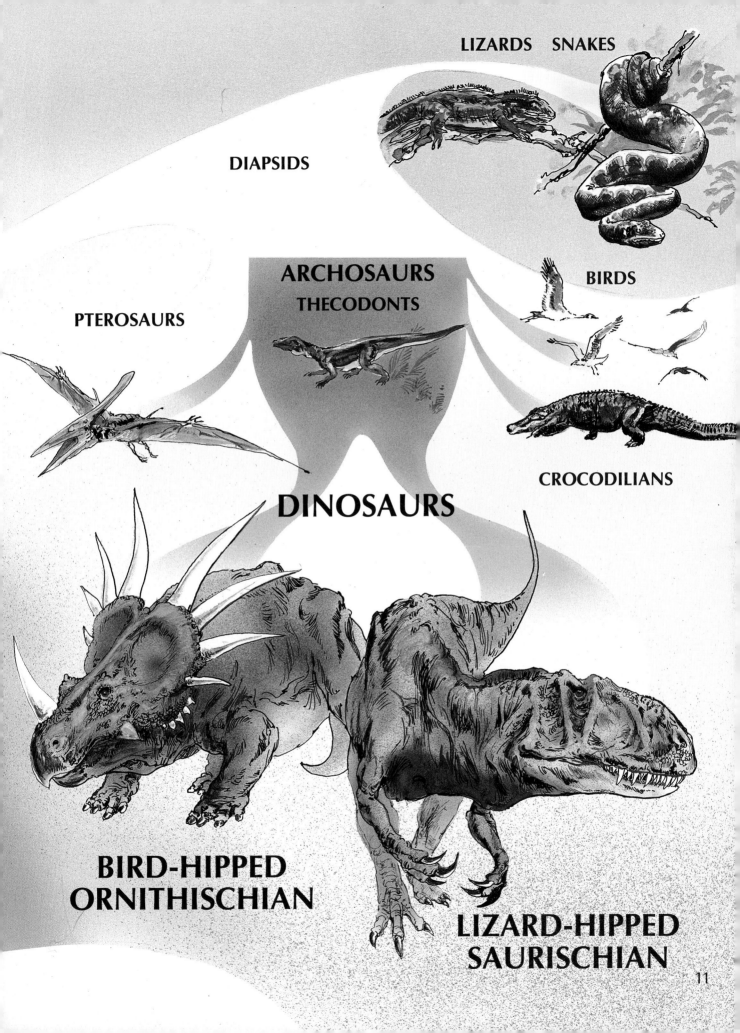

LIZARDS   SNAKES

DIAPSIDS

ARCHOSAURS
THECODONTS

PTEROSAURS

BIRDS

DINOSAURS

CROCODILIANS

BIRD-HIPPED
ORNITHISCHIAN

LIZARD-HIPPED
SAURISCHIAN

MESOZOIC ERA

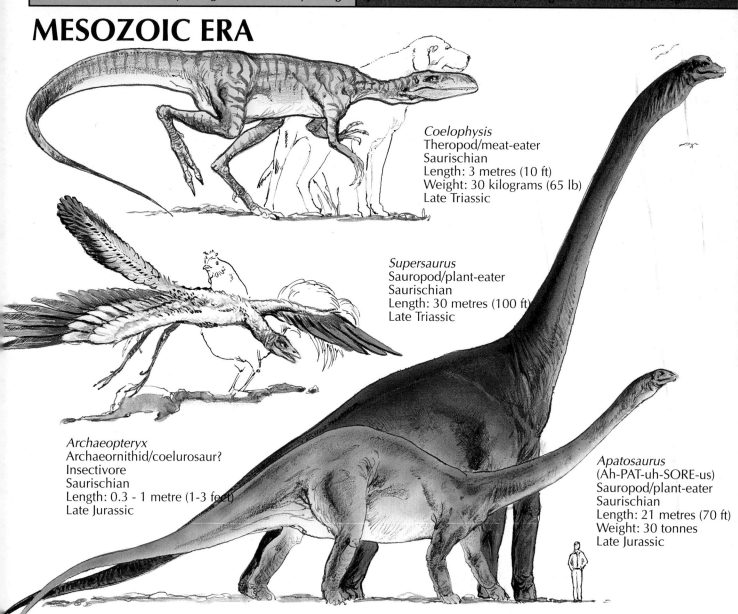

Coelophysis
Theropod/meat-eater
Saurischian
Length: 3 metres (10 ft)
Weight: 30 kilograms (65 lb)
Late Triassic

Supersaurus
Sauropod/plant-eater
Saurischian
Length: 30 metres (100 ft)
Late Triassic

Archaeopteryx
Archaeornithid/coelurosaur?
Insectivore
Saurischian
Length: 0.3 - 1 metre (1-3 feet)
Late Jurassic

Apatosaurus
(Ah-PAT-uh-SORE-us)
Sauropod/plant-eater
Saurischian
Length: 21 metres (70 ft)
Weight: 30 tonnes
Late Jurassic

Two groups of Dinosaurs

When dinosaurs were first named, it was thought that they belonged to a single order of reptiles. Later, a scientist pointed out that the dinosaurs actually included two orders of animals. The difference was in the way the animals' hips were made. Some had hips like those of birds. Others had hips like lizards'. These two groups also differed in the size of the holes in their skulls and in the way their teeth were arranged.

The ones with the bird hips are called **ornithischians** (OR-nih-THISS-chee-uns). Those with lizard hips are called **saurischians** (Sore-ISS-chee-uns). Even within these two orders of dinosaurs there are many suborders. The creatures in each group varied greatly in size, speed, intelligence, and living habits. The bird-hipped dinosaurs all had one thing in common—they were all plant-eaters. Plant-eaters are called **herbivores**. The lizard-hipped dinosaurs were made up of both plant-eaters and meat-eaters. Meat-eaters are called **carnivores**.

The Lizard-hipped Dinosaurs

The lizard-hipped, or saurischian dinosaurs include some of the greatest hunters that have ever lived. The terrifying images we have of dinosaurs are mostly of meat-eaters from this group. But not all were towering giants with wicked teeth and claws. Many were specially adapted to live a calm life of eating insects or plants. Even among those that hunted

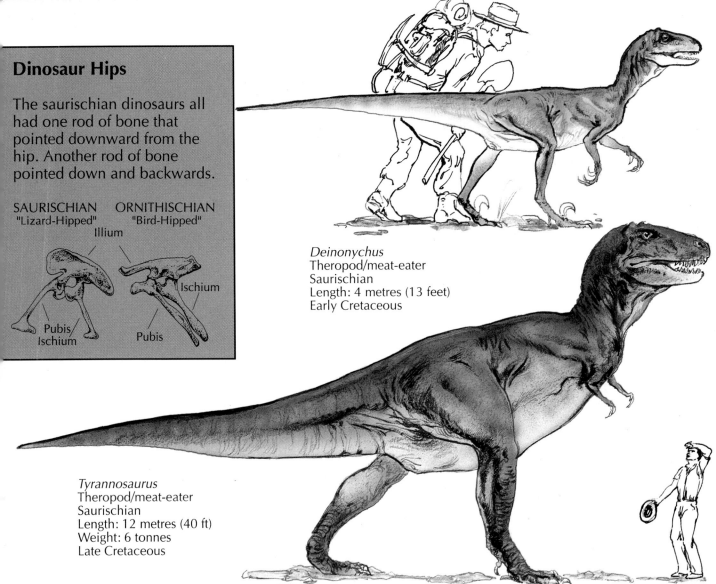

Dinosaur Hips

The saurischian dinosaurs all had one rod of bone that pointed downward from the hip. Another rod of bone pointed down and backwards.

SAURISCHIAN
"Lizard-Hipped"

ORNITHISCHIAN
"Bird-Hipped"

Illium

Ischium

Pubis/
Ischium

Pubis

Deinonychus
Theropod/meat-eater
Saurischian
Length: 4 metres (13 feet)
Early Cretaceous

Tyrannosaurus
Theropod/meat-eater
Saurischian
Length: 12 metres (40 ft)
Weight: 6 tonnes
Late Cretaceous

meat were a surprising number no bigger than a large dog.

The plant-eaters among the lizard-hipped dinosaurs include some of the largest creatures that have ever lived. They were certainly the tallest! Just when scientists think they have found the largest of these animals, it seems a new and larger one is discovered.

Among the lizard-hipped dinosaurs, there were three different body types. The earliest were the **prosauropods** (pro-SORE-uh-pods). These were quite small plant-eaters—that is, quite small compared to the later saurischians! Prosauropods only grew up to 6 metres (20 ft) in length. Most

were rather clumsy and were able to walk either on their hind legs or on all fours. The second lizard-hipped dinosaur group, the sauropods, were their descendants. The sauropods were also plant-eaters. These were the largest of all land animals. The biggest identified so far is thought to have been about 36.5 metres (120 ft) long! This was the giant *Seismosaurus* (SIZE-muh-SORE-us), which was discovered recently in New Mexico.

Much of the sauropods' length came from their long necks and tails. For many years, scientists thought that these creatures spent most of the time in the water.

They thought the long necks were used to hold their heads above the water so they could breathe. But now it is thought that these long necks, like giraffes', were used for nibbling leaves at the tops of trees.

The third group of saurischians were the *theropods* (THAIR-uh-pods). These were the only animals among all the dinosaurs that ate meat. Whether enormous like the ferocious *Tyrannosaurus* (Tie-RAN-uh-SORE-us) or quite small like 4-metre (13-ft) *Deinonychus* (Dine-ON-ik-us), the theropods all had strong hind legs, oversized heads with large jaws, and deadly claws. With this equipment, they were very successful hunters.

13

Tyrannosaurus—The Tyrant Lizard

The herd of duckbills was quietly grazing in the lower marshlands when *Tyrannosaurus* spotted it. It had been four days since her last meal so she was impatient. Usually, she would watch and wait before moving in for the kill. The battle was much easier when she could pick out a weaker animal. Now, however, she rushed ahead out of hunger and excitement.

Her huge bulk crashed its way out of the forest she had been spying from. Her muscular legs carried her quickly into the open. But her 12-metre (40-ft) long body had made plenty of noise. By the time she made her way to the marsh, the alarm had already gone out among her prey. The duckbills dashed for safety. Many went into the water. They knew *Tyrannosaurus* was unlikely to follow them there.

As the last of the herd disappeared, all *Tyrannosaurus* could do was roar out her anger. She was a terrifying sight with her enormous jaws open to show row after row of dagger-like teeth. Some of them were 20 centimetres (8 in) long and had edges like a steak knife. But her intended dinner was off in the distance now. Disappointed, she turned and headed back towards the woods to search for other prey.

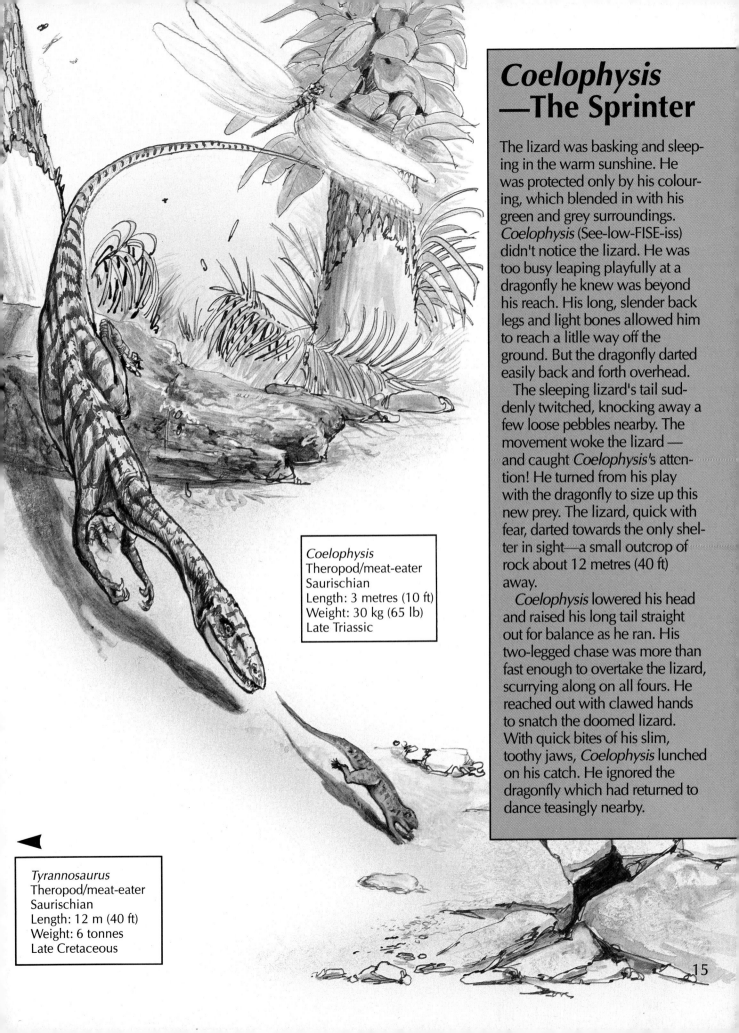

Coelophysis
—The Sprinter

The lizard was basking and sleeping in the warm sunshine. He was protected only by his colouring, which blended in with his green and grey surroundings. *Coelophysis* (See-low-FISE-iss) didn't notice the lizard. He was too busy leaping playfully at a dragonfly he knew was beyond his reach. His long, slender back legs and light bones allowed him to reach a litlle way off the ground. But the dragonfly darted easily back and forth overhead.

The sleeping lizard's tail suddenly twitched, knocking away a few loose pebbles nearby. The movement woke the lizard — and caught *Coelophysis*'s attention! He turned from his play with the dragonfly to size up this new prey. The lizard, quick with fear, darted towards the only shelter in sight—a small outcrop of rock about 12 metres (40 ft) away.

Coelophysis lowered his head and raised his long tail straight out for balance as he ran. His two-legged chase was more than fast enough to overtake the lizard, scurrying along on all fours. He reached out with clawed hands to snatch the doomed lizard. With quick bites of his slim, toothy jaws, *Coelophysis* lunched on his catch. He ignored the dragonfly which had returned to dance teasingly nearby.

Coelophysis
Theropod/meat-eater
Saurischian
Length: 3 metres (10 ft)
Weight: 30 kg (65 lb)
Late Triassic

Tyrannosaurus
Theropod/meat-eater
Saurischian
Length: 12 m (40 ft)
Weight: 6 tonnes
Late Cretaceous

Archaeopteryx
Archaeornithid/coelurosaur?
Insectivore
Saurischian
Length: 0.3 - 1 metre (1-3 ft)
Late Jurassic

Archaeopteryx —Ancient Wing

Archaeopteryx (Ar-kee-OP-ter-ix) was perched in the lower branches of a tall conifer. She was lazily preening her feathers. Stretching out one long wing, she pecked at the mites that were burrowing into her skin. Their tiny bodies crunched easily in her tooth-filled jaws. But they were not enough to satisfy her hunger.

Below her were the remains of a baby sauropod. It had been almost stripped to the bone by a pack of meat-eaters earlier that day. She knew that the body would already have attracted a host of flies and other insects she could feed on. But to leave her perch in the tree would be risky. Once she was on the ground, her weak wings would not allow her to escape danger quickly. Soon, however, her hunger got the better of her. She clumsily made her way step by step to the outer edge of the branch she was on. Her hind toe curved backwards, giving her a sure grasp. A second pair of claws on her wings pushed overhead branches out of her way. Once away from the tangle of branches, she spread her wings and hopped up off her perch. At first, she seemed to drop straight towards the ground. But soon an air draught caught her from below. By tipping her wings this way and that, she managed to fall more or less near the sauropod's body. She hopped over to the carcass and nudged the head upwards with her beak-like jaw. Sure enough, a scurrying mass of long black beetles was underneath. She could also see grubs and maggots already nestling in the open rib cage. She looked around for signs of danger. Her only company was a group of small mammals. They would compete for insects, but would not harm her. Happily, she set into her meal.

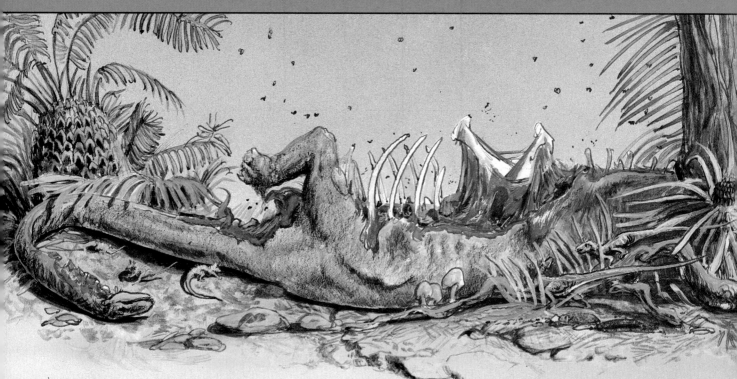

Diplodocus
Sauropod/ plant-eater
Saurischian
Length: 27.5 m (90 ft)
Weight: 11 tonnes
Late Jurassic

Diplodocus — A Gentle Giant

The *Diplodocus* (Dih-PLOD-uh-kus) herd had grazed the branches of the cycad forest almost bare. The waste they left behind contained seeds and fertilizer for a new generation of trees. But in the meantime, they had to keep moving. Their huge bodies, weighing up to 11 tonnes, demanded constant feeding.

With their great size and whip-like tails, the giant sauropods faced few enemies. But the wide trail of stripped and broken forest was a clear map for any meat-eater that might follow. At that moment, a lone *Allosaurus*, the fiercest hunter of his time, had come across the clearing where the *Diplodocus* herd had fed the day before. Although they had covered a fair distance since then, the *Allosaurus*'s upright stance would allow him to catch up soon. Alone, separated from his pack, *Allosaurus* stood little chance against an adult *Diplodocus*. But perhaps if he could catch a young one trailing behind...

Allosaurus came upon the herd a few hours later. He waited downwind from them, keeping an eye on the weaker members. As he watched, the herd suddenly stopped feeding and looked in his direction. He had been spotted! Quickly, the sauropods arranged themselves in a protective wall. The young and the weak were hidden behind the enormous bulk of healthy adults. With tails lashing in fear and anger, the *Diplodocus* herd waited. Even without claws and with only blunt teeth for chewing plants, they were a fearsome challenge for the hunter.

Frustrated, *Allosaurus* retreated. As he backed off along the trail, the *Diplodocus* herd returned to the important job of feeding.

The Bird-hipped Dinosaurs

The lizard-hipped dinosaurs may have included the largest and the fiercest. The ornithischians, or bird-hipped dinosaurs, included some of the strangest. This group of dinosaurs developed an amazing range of features to protect and to identify themselves. These features included horns, frills, spikes, plates, and crests. Because the ornithischians were all plant-eaters, they had powerful jaws for grinding, and flat teeth that were well adapted to chewing.

But their jaws and teeth were not much use against attackers.

The earliest bird-hipped dinosaurs were the ornithopods (or-NITH-uh-pods), or bird-footed, dinosaurs. These appeared during the Late Triassic Period. The second branch of this order of dinosaurs was the curious stegosaurs (STEG-uh-sores). These slow, four-footed creatures had large triangular plates along their backs. These plates may have helped protect them from other animals. They may also have helped them to control their body temperature.

The greatest number of bird-hipped dinosaurs appeared in the Late Cretaceous Period, the

final age of dinosaurs. At this time, fierce meat-eating predators such as *Tyrannosaurus* roamed the earth. The great variety of physical features that the bird-hipped dinosaurs developed may have been to protect them.

There were four main groups of ornithischians during the Late Cretaceous Period. The **hadrosaurs** (HAD-ruh-sores), or "duckbills", were medium-sized dinosaurs that lived in marshlands and forests. They are called duckbills because their jaws resembled ducks' beaks. Many different species of duckbills had strange crests on top of their heads. These crests may have helped the duckbills to

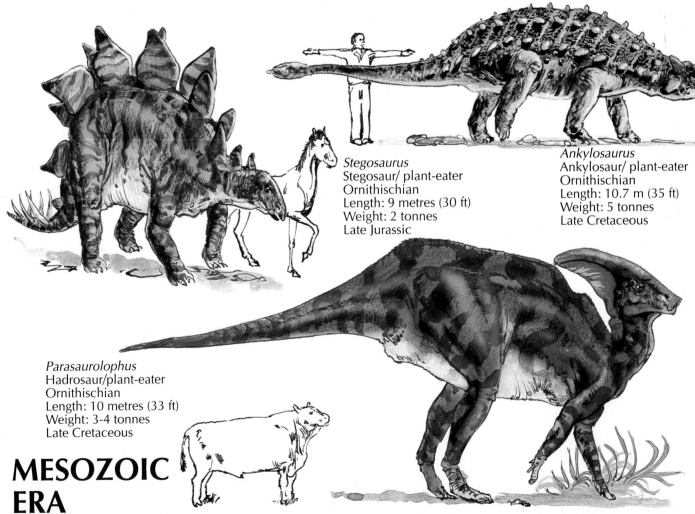

Stegosaurus
Stegosaur/ plant-eater
Ornithischian
Length: 9 metres (30 ft)
Weight: 2 tonnes
Late Jurassic

Ankylosaurus
Ankylosaur/ plant-eater
Ornithischian
Length: 10.7 m (35 ft)
Weight: 5 tonnes
Late Cretaceous

Parasaurolophus
Hadrosaur/plant-eater
Ornithischian
Length: 10 metres (33 ft)
Weight: 3-4 tonnes
Late Cretaceous

MESOZOIC ERA

TRIASSIC 225 million years ago to 195 million years ago | **JURASSIC** 195 million years ago to 136 million years ago

know their own group or to alert others to danger.

The ankylosaurs (ang-KILE-uh-sores) were another squat, heavy group like the stegosaurs. Their backs were covered in armour-like plates. They also had thick clubs of bone and wicked spikes on their tails for protection.

The ceratopsians (kair-uh-TOP-see-uns), or horned dinosaurs, were a match even for *Tyrannosaurus*. Different species of ceratopsians had different numbers of horns jutting from their heads. All of them had a wide, bony frill behind the head to protect the neck. They also had hooked snouts for nipping off leaves and which could also have been used for digging nests for their eggs. The last and strangest of the bird-hipped dinosaurs were the pachycephalosaurs (pack-ee-KEF-uh-low-sores), or "bone-heads". These odd creatures had heads that were enormous compared to their bodies. Some species had skulls that were twenty times thicker than ours! All of this was to protect their tiny brains. They may have used their thick skulls for fierce head-bashing contests.

Triceratops
Ceratopsian/plant-eater
Ornithischian
Length: 9 metres (30 ft)
Weight 4-6 tonnes
Late Cretaceous

Pachycephalosaurus
Ornithopod/plant-eater
Ornithischian
Length: 4.6 metres (15 ft)
Weight: 2-3 tonnes
Late Cretaceous

Ouranosaurus
(Our-AN-uh-SORE-us)
Ornithopod
Ornithischian
Length: 7 metres (23 ft)
Weight: 1 tonne
Early Cretaceous

CRETACEOUS 136 million years ago to 65 million years ago

Triceratops —A Battle to the Death

With the dry weather, the horned dinosaurs found fewer and fewer plants to eat on the plains. The few trees and plants that remained were too bitter and tough even for their powerful jaws. So, as they had done for generations, they began to migrate. They headed in the direction from which the wettest winds blew.

As always, the herd moved together in protective formation. The young and weaker members kept towards the inside. The healthy adults formed a wall of jutting horns and brightly coloured frills that would impress even the largest enemies.

The carnosaurs of the region were familiar with mighty *Triceratops* (Try-KAIR-uh-tops). Many had died on their horns, so they usually kept their distance. In good times, there was plenty of weaker prey to feed on. But the **drought** had already driven many of the plant-eating herds onward to look for food. Many carnivores had followed. They were fierce with hunger.

A pack of *Tyrannosaurus* came upon the *Triceratops* as they travelled. The meat-eaters attacked from the rear. The first to move in were quickly gored on the three horns of the adults' heads. But while the front line of *Triceratops* was engaged in battle, other *Tyrannosaurus* had rushed in to attack the weaker ones. Their huge jaws clamped around the ribs of the smaller members. A few *Triceratops* were carried off before the attackers drew back. Several of the meat-eaters limped from great gashes to their legs. Many more had died. But at least there would be meat for the survivors.

The *Triceratops* regrouped. The herd was smaller now, but still strong. They continued their trek toward the wetlands.

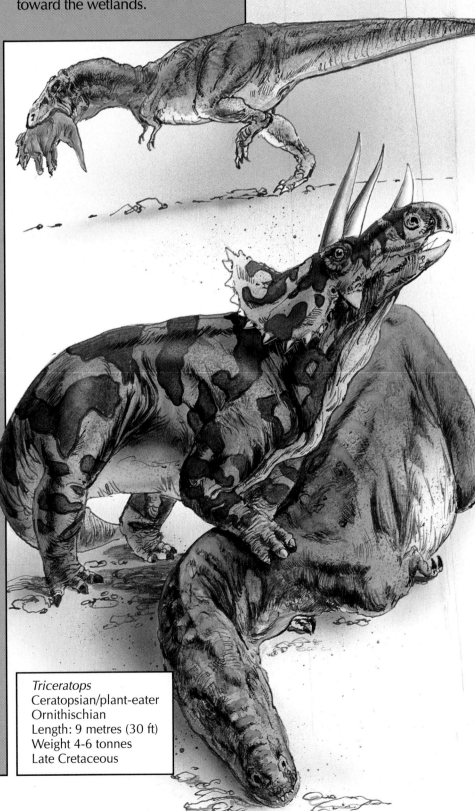

Triceratops
Ceratopsian/plant-eater
Ornithischian
Length: 9 metres (30 ft)
Weight 4-6 tonnes
Late Cretaceous

Stegosaurus and *Ankylosaurus*—The Armoured Tanks

Although they lived a long time apart, these two dinosaurs seemed to have the same idea about how to survive—wear plenty of armour!

Stegosaurus wore a row of triangle-shaped plates down the centre of his back. These may have been helpful in controlling his body temperature. In cool weather, they might have caught the rays of the sun. In warm weather, the wind flowing around the plates might have cooled the blood in them. The plates also made *Stegosaurus* look bigger. That might have scared off some meat-eaters. If his back plates weren't enough to discourage a hungry predator, *Stegosaurus* still had the long spikes on his tail to defend himself with.

Ankylosaurus, which came later, also depended on armour to protect her from hungry jaws. This slow-moving plant-eater had a round back that was completely covered in plates, spikes, and bony ridges. If attacked, she probably just sat down and waved her mighty clubbed tail. Even the jaws of *Tyrannosaurus* would have found her armour tough to chew on.

Stegosaurus
Stegosaur/ plant-eater
Ornithischian
Length: 9 m (30 ft)
Weight: 2 tonnes
Late Jurassic

Ankylosaurus
Ankylosaur/ plant-eater
Ornithischian
Length: 10.7 m (35 ft)
Weight: 5 tonnes
Late Cretaceous

21

Parasaurolophus—A Stray Duckbill

The young female was wandering lost along the forest's edge, keeping close to the shore of the lake. Without the protection of her herd, she knew that her only hope of escaping danger would be to take to the water.

Earlier that day, the herd had been attacked and broken up by a pack of hunting carnivores. At first the *Parasaurolophus* (Par-uh-sore-OL-uh-fus) herd had taken flight together, and headed for the lake waters. But the meat-eaters had attacked from two sides, throwing the herd into confusion. She had been one of the lucky ones — strong and fast enough to escape. Others had fallen to the claws and teeth of the hunters.

As she moved along the water's edge, the *Parasaurolophus* grazed on low-lying shrubs, marsh grasses, and the lower branches of trees. She chewed easily with her many rows of teeth. From time to time, she rose up on her hind legs and sniffed the air, hoping to catch the scent of others of her kind. The tubes that ran into the long curved crest on her head were connected to her nose. Her sense of smell was keen.

Sure enough, as daylight was fading, she smelled the familiar odour that told her she was downwind from her herd. Happily, she let loose a cry that echoed through the crest. Its deep sound carried up the shore to her brothers and sisters. They bellowed a reply that she knew could only come from her own kind. It told her where they were and that it was safe. Quickly but carefully, she made her way along the shore to the safety of the herd.

Parasaurolophus
Hadrosaur/plant-eater
Ornithischian
Length: 10 m (33 feet)
Weight: 3-4 tonnes
Late Cretaceous

Pachycephalosaurus
Ornithopod/plant-eater
Ornithischian
Length: 4.6 metres (15 ft)
Weight: 2-3 tonnes
Late Cretaceous

The Challenge—*Pachycephalosaurus*

The fight had been going on for hours. The young male was depending on his greater strength to outlast his opponent. The older male was feeling the strain of the battle. His shoulders and hind legs were aching. But experience could still win out over youth. He had defeated many younger males in his time.

Once again, their heads came together with a thunderous crash. Any other animal would have been killed by such a blow. But *Pachycephalosaurus*'s tiny brain was protected by a skull 25 centimetres (10 in) thick. Blood streamed down both of their heads, but their lives were in no danger.

Tiring of the fight, the older **bonehead** would try to put a quick end to things. With every new charge, each opponent would move back a few paces, rear up on hind legs, and aim his head at the other's skull. This time, the older male brought his head down lower, almost to the ground. As the younger one's head went back over his shoulder, the elder one raised his club-like head. The blow caught his opponent squarely under the jaw, knocking him backwards. Stunned, the young *Pachycephalosaurus* lay for an instant on his side. The elder one took his advantage and butted him again and again on the ribs. Bellowing in pain, the young bonehead staggered to his feet and backed away, shaking his head in surrender.

The elder would continue to lead the herd for another season. He honked out his victory to the females that were grazing in the distance. Disinterested, they continued to eat, gently butting each other from time to time.

Where Dinosaurs Lived

Most of the knowledge we have about where and how dinosaurs lived comes from the bones that scientists have found. Most dinosaur bones have been found at the sites of ancient river-beds. Flash floods may have caused many dinosaurs to die all at the same time in these spots. Disasters like these could have left behind the huge dinosaur graveyards full of bones that scientists have found in some areas.

But scientists cannot be completely certain about where some dinosaurs lived. Bones might have been carried down the river from their original sites. Drought might have caused some herds to migrate from their usual homes to the river sites in search of food and water. As regions dried up, many species may have died together in areas where they did not usually live. With some species, scientists have only found the remains of one or two individual dinosaurs. It is often difficult for scientists to decide how much information about the whole species these few fossils can tell us.

What scientists can usually tell from fossils is the species of dinosaur they are from and roughly where that species lived. The map on page 25 shows where a number of different dinosaurs' fossils have been found so far. These dinosaurs might also have lived in other parts of the world where their bones have not yet been found. Remember that the continents of the world have moved since some of these creatures lived. The countries and climates they are found in have changed greatly since the times in which they lived.

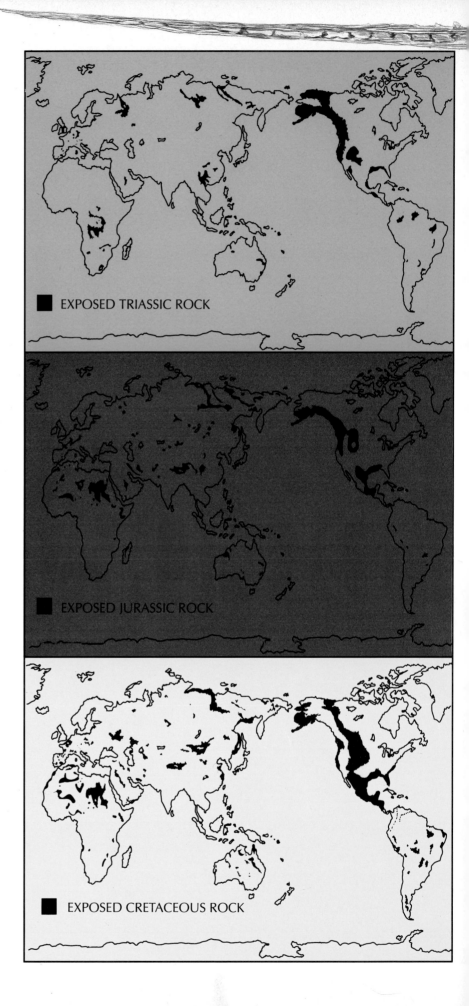

EXPOSED TRIASSIC ROCK

EXPOSED JURASSIC ROCK

EXPOSED CRETACEOUS ROCK

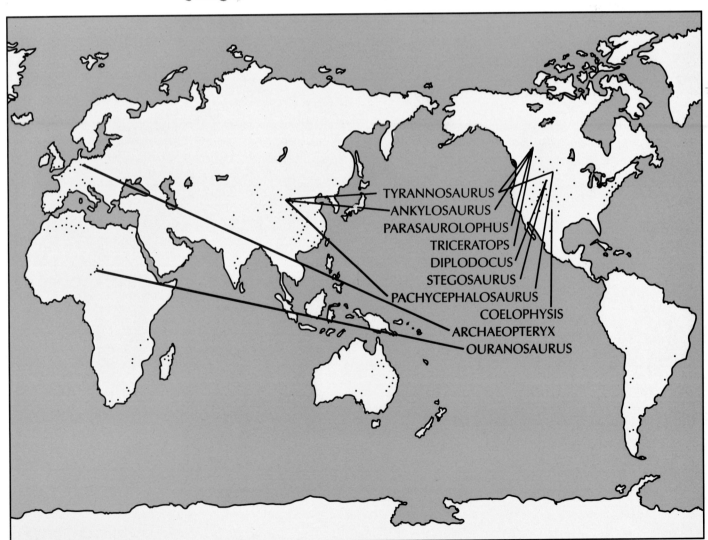

TYRANNOSAURUS
ANKYLOSAURUS
PARASAUROLOPHUS
TRICERATOPS
DIPLODOCUS
STEGOSAURUS
PACHYCEPHALOSAURUS
COELOPHYSIS
ARCHAEOPTERYX
OURANOSAURUS

Finding Dinosaurs Today

Dinosaur fossils have been found all over the world. Some areas have proven richer in bones than others. But we have only begun to look. Other areas of the world will almost certainly produce great numbers of dinosaur fossils.

The process of finding, uncovering, and shipping dinosaur bones is very difficult and expensive. The bones are often found in layers of rock that may be harder than the bones themselves. Usually, the dinosaur skeletons are in many pieces. Scientists have to be extremely careful in removing the bones from the rock so that important pieces are not lost or damaged. The scientists must often start their work with dynamite to break up the hard rock. Then they can use smaller and smaller tools to remove the bones.

Once the dinosaur bones have been dug up, they are numbered so that they can be taken apart, shipped, and then put back together again. The bones are sent to natural history museums, where specially trained people begin the long process of sorting out the bones and rebuilding complete skeletons. If pieces are missing, these people will borrow bones from other skeletons or make them from plaster. From the skeleton, scientists can tell a lot about how heavy the dinosaur might have been, how it might have walked, what it ate, and many other things. They can build life-sized models of the creatures that look real enough to move! One thing that we don't know very much about is the colour of dinosaurs. Fossils tell us little about the dinosaurs' outsides.

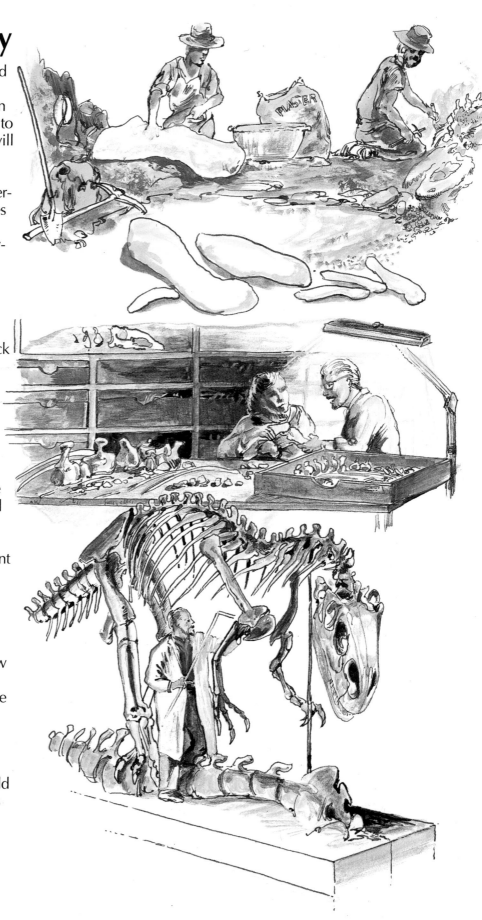

Dentists' Tools on Dinosaur Hunts?

Separating hard rock from hard bone can be a very delicate job. Very fine tools have to be used so the fossils won't be damaged. Dental tools such as these drills and picks, are often used when the larger pieces of rock have been removed.

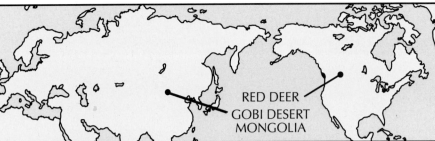

OTHNIEL CHARLES MARSH

EDWARD DRINKER COPE

ROY CHAPMAN ANDREWS

Fossil Hunts

About half of all species of dinosaurs that have been found so far come from Alberta in Canada, and the Gobi Desert in Mongolia. Thirty-five different species have been found so far in the Red Deer River Valley region of Alberta. All of the animals found seem to be from the last fifteen million years of dinosaur life.

The parched desert of Inner Mongolia was explored in the 1920s and 1930s by teams from France, Sweden, and the United States. In 1922, an American team uncovered the first dinosaur eggs. They were the eggs of *Protoceratops*. The American team also found the skulls of seven little creatures that proved that small mammals lived alongside the dinosaurs.

Great numbers of dinosaurs were also discovered in the 1870s in the western United States. These finds were the result of a fierce competition between two American dinosaur collectors. The two men, Othniel Charles Marsh and Edward Drinker Cope, competed to identify the greatest number of dinosaurs. In many ways, their competing caused problems for science, but it certainly uncovered many new dinosaurs.

Even now, new searches are taking place that will reveal new dinosaurs. Scientists are once again looking into the rich fossil fields of China and Canada. What they find will provide new pieces to fit into the great dinosaur mystery puzzle.

RED DEER
GOBI DESERT
MONGOLIA

What would Dinosaurs look like Today?

Just why the dinosaurs vanished sixty-five million years ago is a mystery. In a very short space of time, nearly all the great land animals and many large sea creatures disappeared from the face of the earth. Scientists once thought that this was a dead end for the dinosaurs. No animal alive today was thought to be related to these ancient giants.

HERON

PROTOAVIS

ARCHAEOPTERYX

TROÖDON

Spot a Dinosaur—Look Up!

New evidence points to a very unlikely modern "grandchild" for the dinosaurs. Birds may well have evolved from the quick and agile meat-eating dinosaurs like *Coelophysis*.

When *Archaeopteryx* was first discovered, scientists thought the skeleton was of a small, two-legged dinosaur. But its wings and feathers were clearly bird-like. *Archaeopteryx* seemed to be half-bird and half-dinosaur. Its claws, long tail, and toothy jaws were those of a reptile. But along with wings and feathers, *Archaeopteryx* had a wishbone collarbone which is only found in birds.

Many scientists still feel that *Archaeopteryx* arrived too late to be the ancestor of modern birds. Real birds appeared too soon after *Archaeopteryx* to have evolved from it. But other skeletons have been found that could link dinosaurs with today's birds. A dinosaur called *Protoavis* (Pro-toe-AV-iss), which means "first bird", was reported in 1986. It is seventy-five million years older than *Archaeopteryx*, and so might have developed later into the early herons and gulls that appeared in the Cretaceous Period. The brain case of a very intelligent late dinosaur, called *Troödon*, also has a feature found in modern birds.

28

Dinosaurs Alive and Well?

From time to time, people report seeing large, terrifying creatures that look like dinosaurs or other ancient giants. There have been tales of a giant creature living in the swamps of central Africa. Could it be a great sauropod like *Diplodocus*? Teams went to search for the creature. They battled weeds and snakes and insects. One searcher said he saw the creature and took its picture. The photo did not develop.

For centuries, people have reported a great snake-like monster living in Loch Ness in Scotland. From the descriptions, it seemed like a plesiosaur —one of the giant sea creatures with turtle-like paddles and very long necks. Many expeditions have looked for "Nessie". Some have even taken photographs, which show dark mounds rising from the water. Perhaps these creatures are survivors of the dinosaur days. Or perhaps they are the products of active imaginations.

Dinosaur Hunter

If we could build a machine that could take us back in time, a visit to the last days of the dinosaurs would be possible. Imagine yourself in a forest seventy-five million years ago. You might find yourself behind an enormous palm tree, quietly watching a family of carnosaurs.

Four youngsters are at play, rolling on the grass and nipping each other with razor-sharp teeth. Small tree ferns crash to the ground under their weight. The two parents are just behind. They are busy tearing apart the carcass of a freshly killed sauropod.

Carefully, you step forward to take a closer look. A tree branch snaps under your foot. And suddenly, six pairs of eyes are staring hungrily at you...

Glossary

adaptation The process of changing to fit an environment.

amphibian Cold-blooded animal that lives part of its life on land, and part in water.

archosaur Dominant reptile group that the dinosaurs descended from.

bonehead Common name for the pachycephalosaurs, a group of duck-billed dinosaurs with very thick skulls.

carnivore Meat-eater.

ceratopsian Group of horned dinosaurs; included *Triceratops*, *Monoclonius*, and others.

climate The year-round weather conditions of a region.

coniferous Cone-bearing trees.

continent Any of the earth's main bodies of land: Europe, Asia, Africa, America, Antarctica, or Australia.

Cretaceous Period The period of history between 136 and 65 million years ago.

cycad Seed-bearing plant similar to a palm tree.

diapsid Ancient group of reptiles that had two skull holes; group of reptiles from which the archosaurs came.

drought Long, dry period.

environment The conditions that surround us.

evolution The slow process by which a species changes.

fossil Plant or animal remains hardened in rock.

Gondwanaland Ancient northern continent that formed when Pangaea, the single land mass, split in two.

hadrosaur Group of dinosaurs known as the duckbills because their jaws resembled ducks' bills.

herbivore Plant-eater

ichthyosaur Ancient ocean reptile that lived between the Triassic and Cretaceous Periods; resembled a dolphin.

Jurassic Period The period in history between 195 and 136 million years ago.

Laurasia Ancient southern continent that formed when Pangaea, the single land mass, split in two.

Mesozoic Era Earth's middle years; period in history between 225 and 65 million years ago.

migration The process of moving from one region to another.

ornithischian The bird-hipped suborder of dinosaurs.

Pangaea The ancient single continent that existed when all of earth's land was joined together.

plesiosaur Large ocean reptile of earth's middle years; resembled a large turtle with a snake-like neck.

pterosaur Order of flying reptiles of the Jurassic and Cretaceous Periods.

prosauropod/sauropod Large, plant-eating lizard-hipped group of dinosaurs.

reptile Cold-blooded, egg-laying animal with a backbone.

saurischian The lizard-hipped suborder of dinosaurs.

synapsid Mammal-like reptiles that died out with the rise of the dinosaurs.

thecodont Group of crocodile-like reptiles that evolved from the archosaurs and led to the dinosaurs.

Triassic Period Period in history between 225 and 195 million years ago.